At David C Cook, we equip the local church around the corner and around the globe to make disciples. Come see how we are working together—go to **www.davidccook.org**. Thank you!

DAVID **C** COOK

*transforming lives together*

# SAY
# YES
## WHEN LIFE
## SAYS NO

### WORKBOOK

DeFOREST B. SOARIES, JR.

# SAY YES

## WHEN LIFE

### SAYS NO

WORKBOOK

DAVID C COOK

*transforming lives together*

SAY YES WHEN LIFE SAYS NO WORKBOOK
Published by David C Cook
4050 Lee Vance Drive
Colorado Springs, CO 80918 U.S.A.

Integrity Music Limited, a Division of David C Cook
Brighton, East Sussex BN1 2RE, England

The graphic circle C logo is a registered trademark of David C Cook.

The website addresses recommended throughout this book are offered as a
resource to you. These websites are not intended in any way to be or imply an
endorsement on the part of David C Cook, nor do we vouch for their content.

Unless otherwise noted, all Scripture quotations are taken from THE
HOLY BIBLE, NEW INTERNATIONAL VERSION®, NIV® Copyright
© 1973, 1978, 1984, 2011 by Biblica, Inc.® Used by permission. All
rights reserved worldwide. Scripture quotations marked KJV are taken
from the King James Version of the Bible. (Public Domain.)

ISBN 978-0-8307-7732-7
eISBN 978-0-8307-7775-4

The Team: Alice Crider, Jeff Gerke, Rachael Stevenson,
Kayla Fenstermaker, Susan Murdock
Cover Design: James Hershberger

Printed in the United States of America
First Edition 2019

1 2 3 4 5 6 7 8 9 10

041719

*This workbook is dedicated to the memory of my teacher and mentor, Dr. Samuel DeWitt Proctor.*

# CONTENTS

# ACKNOWLEDGMENTS

Many great influences in my life contributed to this workbook becoming reality. I am grateful to God for all of them—my parents, my church families, my employers, and my teachers. The Bible has been the most influential book in my life, followed by the works of many great authors—Rick Warren, Gordon MacDonald, Tim Keller, Stephen R. Covey, David J. Schwartz, Charles Duhigg, Darren Hardy, and Juliet Schor.

Because of the positive impact these authors have had on me, I have committed significant time to writing, hoping that I can help others similarly. Aiding me in this effort are people whose roles are indispensable: my wife, Donna; my writing assistant, Jen DaSilva; my capable operations coordinator, Michelle Charles; and my transcriber, Angela Dadson.

A special thanks to the many people who participated in our thirty-one-day makeover experience that was the basis for this workbook. Their comments and feedback contributed significantly to the final form of this project.

This workbook would not have become reality without the support, guidance, and critique of the outstanding editorial team at David C Cook, including Alice Crider and Jeff Gerke. Their participation throughout the publishing process helped my work make so much more sense than it otherwise would have. Special thanks to them.

I am thankful most of all to God for granting me the privilege of sharing what I possess with those who can benefit from my sharing. Thank God for the grace that makes my life and ministry possible.

# INTRODUCTION

*There is a time for everything, and a season*
*for every activity under the heavens.*

Ecclesiastes 3:1

Whenever I experience something positive, I try to share it with others. In John 9, I discovered a man who was born blind and was healed by Jesus. After I was diagnosed with cancer, I thought perhaps this man could teach me how to access the healing power of Jesus.

What ended up happening was that Mr. Blind Man, as I like to refer to him, taught me to make some key decisions and take some needed actions, even though Jesus has the power to do anything for me. This blind man's teachings changed my life. He taught me to say yes when life says no.

After learning these principles, I worked to apply them to my entire life. I used a systematic process to do this. And while I don't believe in being a slave to a system, I do think it's not enough to have principles without having a concrete approach to using those principles. So I have summarized my own practices in this workbook.

The best way to use this workbook is in a thirty-one-day process that includes life-changing exercises and decisions. This workbook will introduce you to a season of self-discovery that I think you will benefit from greatly. The material you learn here lends itself to being regularly reviewed, and your plans and goals can be updated on a regular basis. This journey may even involve you sharing with a coach or a small group. As a companion to *Say Yes When Life Says No*, this workbook will become as helpful to you as the blind man of John 9 was to me so you can be equipped to say yes when life says no.

God bless you as you launch into this new season of your life.

---

# NOW OR NEVER

*Show me, LORD, my life's end and the number of*
*my days; let me know how fleeting my life is.*

Psalm 39:4

I am at a stage in my life when it is critical to have a specific plan for my future. I have some "now or never" items on my list of dreams. Actually this is not really new. Every season in life is critical, and every dream should be approached as a "now or never" undertaking. I wish I had learned that earlier in life.

Welcome to your thirty-one-day makeover!

Every journey begins when you determine the destination. The road to success begins with setting goals. Goals with real value have a timetable included. A goal without a deadline is just a dream. I have always achieved more when I have given myself a deadline.

Here's how I look at it: either I will be alive after a certain date (the deadline) or I will not. It sounds very simple, but putting the future into those terms always positions me to hope for the best, prepare for the worst, and set goals for both.

It is possible to experience tremendous success in thirty-one days. In the past, I have lost a lot of weight in thirty-one days, I have had surgery to remove cancer from my body thirty-one days after being diagnosed, and I have written a book in thirty-one days. Thirty-one days is 744 hours, which is a lot of time. If we spend it wisely and aim at specific goals, we can all achieve great results in 744 hours!

Today is the first day of your thirty-one-day journey. The task today is to set your goal for the first day of the next month. For example, if you're starting this workbook on July 1, you will set your goal achievement date for August 1.

Remember, either you will be here on your goal achievement day or you will not. To prepare for the possibility of not being here, you should get your house in order. This is not to be morbid—it is just reality.

The other possibility is that you *will* be alive on your goal achievement day. Since most of us plan to be here in thirty-one days, we should be asking ourselves at least one of these questions: Who will I be after day 31? What will I have after day 31 that I currently don't have? What will I accomplish between now and the last day of this journey?

A proverb says the journey of a thousand miles begins with one step. The first step for Mr. Blind Man was to leave his house to beg. His first step led to his miraculous healing.

The first step for you is to paint a picture of yourself—at least write a sentence about yourself—that describes what and who you want to see when you look in the mirror after day 31.

Today the task is to become as focused as possible on who you want to become. This is your giant goal for the whole project. The clearer your vision for yourself, the easier the strategy for getting there will be.

## ACTION ITEMS

1. Identify your goal, and write down at least one thing you will start doing, have in your possession, or complete by the end of thirty-one days.

2. Place your written goal in a sealed envelope, and ask someone you trust to give it to you on day 28.

3. Make sure you are prepared for the unlikely event of an early departure from this life. Write down what you have prepared for in the event of an early departure. Do you have a medical directive and written will? Are all your personal business documents organized and accessible to someone who will handle your affairs? Have you established a personal relationship with God to ensure your eternal security?

Let's go!

---

# A COMPLETE LIFE

*"The thief comes only to steal and kill and destroy; I have
come that they may have life, and have it to the full."*

John 10:10

Whenever I take my car for servicing, the staff always checks a complete list of items to ensure the vital parts of the car are working.
Even if my concern is limited to a particular part of the car or if I
simply want my oil changed, those responsible for keeping my car
in working order insist on checking everything on their list. They
understand that if the entire car is not functioning properly, the one
part having difficulty may just be the proverbial tip of the iceberg.
I have learned to allow them to take as much time as they need,
even if that's more time than I would like. And I have my entire car
checked every few thousand miles.

   This same approach is useful in my life. If my car needs a complete checkup on a regular basis, then my life deserves at least what
my car deserves. I probably will not have my car for the rest of my

life, but I will have my life for the rest of my life! So I give my whole life a maintenance check on a regular basis.

This sounds a bit overwhelming—and it was for me at first. But I was making the mistake of trying to improve my life by focusing only on the area that had the greatest need. That seemed to make so much sense. What I learned was that while the area of need was getting all the attention, the areas that had relatively little need were getting no attention at all. By the time I had fixed the needy area, some other area was in need. And the cycle never ended.

These days, I spend most of my spare time helping people understand and improve their financial condition. The first objective is always to get them out of debt. That is where I started when I was determined to repair my finances. So long as I was drowning in debt, I could never save, invest, or donate money.

As with my car, simply focusing on the problem area in your life—finances, for example—is not really an effective way to solve your financial challenges. We have to consider every aspect of our lives.

I ultimately discovered that the best strategy was to set goals and improve my whole life rather than just the one area that gave me the most concern. This meant that I had to organize my life into a checklist of areas and create a plan for each. The system I have embraced divides my life into five categories: personal, intellectual, vocational, financial, and spiritual.

To address one of these areas without working on the others is to develop an unbalanced life. Filling out the entire checklist guarantees that I am building a complete life. As you proceed this month, this workbook will help you build a complete life using this system.

# ACTION ITEMS

1. Make a general list of the issues you face or the parts of your life that are important to you (e.g., exercise, rest, prayer, debt, friendships, etc.).

2. Assign each of the items on your list to one of the five categories mentioned above.

| CATEGORY 1: PERSONAL | CATEGORY 2: INTELLECTUAL | CATEGORY 3: VOCATIONAL | CATEGORY4: FINANCIAL | CATEGORY 5: SPIRITUAL |
|---|---|---|---|---|
|  |  |  |  |  |

3. Identify which items you will address this month. List them here.

## DAY 3

# PASSION

*As the deer pants for streams of water, so
my soul pants for you, my God.*

Psalm 42:1

Before I say any more about goals, I want to pause to say a word about passion. Someone once asked me how he could find his passion. I had to think about this for a while because I felt as though I have known my passion all my life. I want to describe passion because I believe we have the best chance of achieving those goals that grow out of our passion.

The word *passion* is used so often that I was tempted to avoid it altogether. Regardless, the concept behind this word is so powerful that if understood properly, it can direct your path for the rest of your life.

My passion is helping people. That's it. Quick and easy to say, and it takes a lifetime to do.

Helping people is also my mission. If I look back over my life, every season has been full of events and activities that all relate to helping others. Sometimes I was more effective at helping people than at other times, and sometimes I enjoyed helping people more than at other times. And sometimes I tried to *not* be passionate about helping people! I finally learned that this is who I am.

The big question for me was how to balance my passion for helping people with my need to take care of my responsibilities and myself. This can be a tremendous challenge. Too often *the things we love to do* and *the things we get paid to do* seem worlds apart. If that reality lasts long enough, we tend to ignore the things we love to do, and we become enslaved to the things we do to survive. At that point we don't even want to be reminded of our passions. Our energy is spent on working to survive.

Finding your passion is critical to your mental health and your quality of life. A person who never finds his or her passion ends up working to fulfill someone else's dreams! Passion is the fuel for the engine of a fulfilled life.

You may be thinking, *What if I don't know what my passion is?* Okay, here's a way to find it: your passion is whatever you would do every day if you didn't need to earn money. Your passion is whatever you enjoy doing so much that you would do it enthusiastically even if someone awakened you at three o'clock in the morning and without warning asked you to do it. Your passion is something you are willing to do although you won't receive any reward from doing it. Your passion is that thing that makes you feel like you've been connected to the purpose for which you were born.

We do best what we love most.

What is your passion? God has created each of us with something on the inside that causes us to feel unfulfilled until we get that "something" out. For me it is helping people through speaking and creating solutions to problems. For my brother it is playing music. What is it for you?

The questions below can help you discover or confirm your passion.

## ACTION ITEMS

1. What would you do if you needed no money at all?

2. Whose life best resembles the life you would like to live?

3. If doing one thing every day would feel fulfilling, what would that be?

## DAY 4

# MISSION

*Trust in the LORD with all your heart and lean not
on your own understanding; in all your ways submit
to him, and he will make your paths straight.*

Proverbs 3:5–6

Today's theme is "mission," so I want to revisit a story to emphasize
the necessity of developing your mission statement.

You may recall that I shared the story of my father's death in
*Say Yes When Life Says No*. I described wearing a brand-new suit and
preparing to leave home for the airport. I was headed to Chicago to
attend the annual fund-raiser for Operation PUSH, where I served
as national coordinator and was about to take on an expanded role
with more responsibilities.

I went to the hospital to check on my dad before leaving for
Chicago, and I discovered an empty room. I thought maybe he had
been transferred to a different section of the hospital. However, my

father had been removed from the room because he had died. We later learned that the anesthesiologist had administered too much anesthesia, and it induced a heart attack that killed him. My father was forty-seven years old.

The pain of losing my father and best friend paralyzed me. As the family grieved the loss of our patriarch, I became overwhelmed by the responsibilities that were now mine as the oldest of three children—the youngest being my eight-year-old sister. That was the darkest day of my life.

We all have dark days. Divorce, criminal conviction, job loss, home foreclosure, business failure, illness, betrayal, and death are just a few experiences that can stop us in our tracks. When you are stopped by circumstances, you can lose your passion. For some people it's only a momentary loss. But some never get it back.

It was my job to write my dad's obituary. As I wrote, I described his accomplishments, but I also felt compelled to describe his character, his beliefs, and his faith. It was not enough to include what he *did* during his life. What became more urgent for me was to let people know who he really *was*—what he stood for and what he believed in. In the end I wanted people to understand that his mission was to be a man of integrity and he had definitely fulfilled his mission across the span of his lifetime.

It was at that very moment, writing my dad's obituary, when I realized I didn't have a mission statement of my own. Your mission describes what you want people to see in you while you're here and what you want people to remember about you when you are gone. It's much more than what you want to have. Your mission describes who you want to be. Without a clear mission, I would remain stuck in my pain or stay busy doing "projects" for the rest of my life. *With* a clear mission, I can stay focused on my purpose for being alive.

When you cannot feel your passion, you can still see your mission!

## ACTION ITEMS

1. In twenty-five words or fewer, write your personal mission statement. If you're not sure how, simply google "Write a mission statement for your life."

2. Write a draft of your own obituary. What would you want said about you at your funeral?

3. Ask someone close to you what he or she thinks your mission is and compare it with your own mission statement.

# THE DIFFERENCE BETWEEN "WHAT" AND "HOW"

*Where there is no revelation, people cast off restraint; but
blessed is the one who heeds wisdom's instruction.*

Proverbs 29:18

Now that you have begun to give serious consideration to your passion and mission, you can begin the process of setting goals. If you have read any of my books on financial freedom and literacy, you may be wondering why this workbook's focus is not getting out of debt. I have said many times that money is one of the things we can use to help us reach our life goals. Debt is one of the barriers that get in our way, but getting out of debt really happens in conjunction with taking control of our entire lives. The way you see and manage life determines the way you understand and handle money. We will definitely discuss finances in this workbook but only after we set the proper framework for the discussion.

Goals are important because they assign specificity to your dreams. All humans dream, and many dreams can come true. Of course, some dreams are pure fantasy, but even your fantastical dreams have kernels of possibility in them.

For example, I had a recurring dream as a child that I could fly. This was probably inspired by my love for television shows like *Superman*. Of course, those dreams were completely ridiculous. In my adult life, though, I have earned so many miles and points on airline frequent flier programs that I have taken many free trips by using airline rewards. I have never grown wings or worn a cape, but I have done an above-average amount of flying. I have spoken in every state in the country and on every continent except Antarctica. Dreams can be taken seriously. Even preposterous dreams can inform our goals.

A goal is a target, a specific intention to accomplish something. Ideally what you want to accomplish is aligned with your mission (see day 4).

When I was a child, President John F. Kennedy announced that America would become the superior nation in conquering outer space. Superiority was the mission. Then we embarked on the goal of putting a man on the moon. Achieving this goal would represent the superiority we sought.

We had to accomplish many tasks in pursuit of that goal—and I call those tasks our objectives. I call my goal the "what," and I call the strategies for achieving my goal the "how."

When you confuse your "what" with your "how," or when you allow your "how" to become your "what," you risk abandoning your "what" when your "how" is disrupted. Let's say reaching a particular destination is my "what" and driving on a certain road is my "how." Now, if the road is blocked because of construction, I don't turn around and go back home. The route I was taking is not my "what"; the route is my "how." So if my "how" is blocked, I simply look for a different road, a detour, or another way to travel to get me where I am going. I keep my "what" and change my "how."

That's why goals are so important. Goals that are written down, as opposed to just being thought or talked about, are critical to achieving success. When I started creating written goals, my life began to soar. Whenever I do one of these thirty-one-day personal makeovers, I start by updating my written goals (beginning with my list of "whats" before I develop my "hows").

## ACTION ITEMS

1.  Considering your mission, make a list of the goals that will help you accomplish it.

2. If any of your goals are "hows" and not "whats," revise or delete them. (Example: Superiority in space was the *mission* of the United States. Putting a man on the moon was the *goal* [what]. *Apollo 11* was the first manned space flight to land on the moon [how]. It could have been *Apollo 12* or *Kennedy 22.* The "how" was the path to achieving the "what," and the "what" supported achieving the mission.)

## DAY 6

# REFLECTION

*When I consider your heavens, the work of your fingers, the moon*
*and the stars, which you have set in place, what is mankind that*
*you are mindful of them, human beings that you care for them?*

Psalm 8:3–4

You are on day 6, and you are beginning to see how time-consuming this process is. Focusing on your own well-being is strenuous work. However, it should not be that way. There is a popular saying that self-preservation is the first law of nature. Maybe it should be natural to identify your passion, update your written goals, and choose what strategies you are going to use to reach your goals. But this practice does not come naturally to many of us.

You are bombarded by nonstop, attention-grabbing messages from marketers who seek your attention, patronage, and loyalty. I can't count the number of television commercials I see, radio ads I hear, newspaper and magazine ads I read, and web-based promotions that fill my inbox. Your consciousness is saturated with commercial noises that fill you with thoughts about everything other than your own welfare.

And your life is busy. You can spend so much time commuting to work, working, preparing for events, attending events, preparing to meet with people, meeting with people, learning and using new technologies, responding to family challenges, doing things for other people, and, of course, shopping. Sometimes you don't have time to make time for yourself. Using time strategically is the key to personal success. It's how you harness your passion.

Before I introduce any more steps into your process, let me invite you to take the time today to reflect and review. You began by identifying one goal you sought to accomplish by the end of this workbook (see day 1). It seems like a long time ago—but it has been only five days! I hope you wrote it down, placed it in an envelope, and asked someone to give it to you on day 28. If you haven't done it yet, now is the time to get that done.

You have also begun writing more of your goals. Although it would be nice to have placed all of them into specific categories, you just want to make sure you have some written goals by now. Look at your goals—make sure they all describe a "what" and not a "how." If you have placed each goal into one of our five categories, you will review each category later on and decide whether the goals are all in the correct categories.

If you have prepared your draft obituary, review it and make any changes that you want to make. If you have not done this yet, don't consider it a morbid activity. We are all going to leave this earth someday. The psalmist asked God to teach him to number his days (see 90:12). Author Stephen Covey said that we should "begin with the end in mind."[1] This kind of advice has helped me for the last twenty years. You will benefit greatly from it.

Today I am pausing to reflect on the commitments and plans I have made this week. I invite you to do likewise.

At the end of the creation week, the Bible says God rested (see Gen. 2:2). But God never needs rest. It may be better to understand God as having reflected on everything He made. That is what day 6 is for us—a day of reflection.

## ACTION ITEMS

1. Consider all your action items to date, and revise any responses you have written for days 1–5.

2. If you have prepared your draft obituary (see day 4), review it and make any changes that you want to make.

3. Did you place your day 1 goal in an envelope? If you have not already done so, do that today. Ask someone to give it to you on day 28.

# NOTE

1. Stephen R. Covey, *The 7 Habits of Highly Effective People: Powerful Lessons in Personal Change* (New York: Simon & Schuster, 2013), 102.

DAY 7

---

# AGE

*I was young and now I am old, yet I have never seen the*
*righteous forsaken or their children begging bread.*

Psalm 37:25

Age is one of the self-imposed barriers that slow us down or even
stop us. I'm not referring to any particular age. I just know from
personal experience that we allow our age to convince us that now
is not the right time to pursue a particular goal. So it's not really our
age—it's our perception of ourselves in light of our age.

A very wise man once told me I should write a book. I dismissed
his advice and told him I was too young to write a book. I didn't
feel I had sufficient experience to be sharing my opinions about
anything with anyone. Who would want advice from someone who
had never really accomplished anything? I liked the idea of writing
a book, but I felt that it was the wrong time ... because of my age.

Years after I'd dismissed the wise man's advice, CNN informed
me that it was going to do a ninety-minute documentary on me, my

church, and our work to help families facing financial hardships. Specifically, they planned to feature my dfree strategy, hoping to motivate other churches to do similar work.

When Soledad O'Brien, the host of the show, shared the news with me, she sternly said, "And you'd better be ready!" In other words, I had to be ready to help people after they saw the documentary. "Ready" meant that I had to write down my philosophy, my strategy, and my program.

It meant I had to write a book.

My response was this—I am too old and too busy to write a book. Isn't that hilarious? First I was too young to be an author; then I was too old. The truth was that I was too something else. I was too insecure, too afraid, too lazy, too undisciplined, too anxious, and too … You name it and I was "too" it! I was using age as an excuse.

Finally I had an amazing realization: no one who has done anything great has been the "ideal" age to do it.

Why? Because there is no ideal age. Greatness almost always occurs at an unlikely age. Or else greatness happens because the great person just ignored his or her age.

Jeremiah thought he was too young to be a prophet (see Jer. 1:6). Abraham and Sarah thought they were too old to have a child (see Gen. 17:17; 18:10–12). Jesus ignored that He was only twelve years old and hung out with the teachers in the temple (see Luke 2:41–46). Stevie Wonder became a star when he was twelve and is still a star more than fifty years later. Ronald Reagan started being president at sixty-nine. Martin Luther King Jr. told the world that he had a dream when he was just thirty-four years old. Laura Stewart, a woman who was a member of Shiloh Baptist Church in Trenton,

New Jersey, when I served as assistant pastor, went to Haiti to start a school while she was in her early nineties. A ninety-four-year-old woman in our church started a new job this year! And a young man in my church started a YouTube channel and had five hundred thousand views when he was sixteen years old.

On the one hand, because I used age as an excuse, you could say I wrote my book—*Say Yes to No Debt*—twenty-five years later than I should have. On the other hand, when I finally did it was the right time too.

Please forget about your age. Stop using it as an excuse. Just decide what you want to accomplish and who you want to be three years from now. I know I am stretching you, but having a vision for the future is vital.

Of course, there are some things your age will not allow you to do. But age is no excuse to have no goals at all. None of us are too young or too old to take control of our futures and pursue our dreams.

## ACTION ITEMS

1. Make sure you have not canceled dreams because of your age. If you have, dust them off and put them back on the list of your active dreams.

2. Place three goals under each of the five goal categories (see day 2).

3. Find someone who is your age and doing something great. Try to make a connection with that individual.

# HELP ME—I'M STUCK!

*Let us not become weary in doing good, for at the proper*
*time we will reap a harvest if we do not give up.*

Galatians 6:9

One thing that surprised me in teaching people to say yes when life says no was encountering so many people who were totally stuck. One person wrote me and said that he couldn't see past his current situation to even set a short-term, one-month goal.

Honestly, though, I have been in that very place. I have been so stuck and so stressed about being stuck that I could not dream, plan, or envision anything ever being different. I was once in such bad shape that while giving a speech to some students at a middle school, I actually stopped speaking, apologized for how bad I was, and promised to return someday when I got my act together. Nothing could be v                         was to be a public speaker!

Here's how I got out of that deep valley. First, I had to admit where I was. I had to admit I was stuck. There is no way to move beyond your present position or condition without honestly admitting where you are. That rule of thumb applies to any situation we encounter. It may be debt, family relations, health, habits, faith, or anything else. It makes no sense to act and think as if everything is all right when it's not. No amount of motivational materials, dynamic sermons, or positive thinking is a substitute for looking in the mirror and admitting that you are stuck. You don't have to broadcast it to others—but you at least have to tell yourself the truth. I made a list of everything in my life that needed to change, every area I was stuck in.

Next, I had to think hard and recapture my dream. Everyone has had a dream. It may require going back to fourth grade when you wanted to be just like your teacher, principal, or pastor. Or it may be when you were in seventh grade and dreamed you would be president of the United States. But every one of us has had at least one dream.

When you remember what it was, the memory alone—or, I should say, the act of remembering—will change your mental state. That may have been your last positive thought, and it may have been completely outlandish, but your future depends completely on your ability to look away from your problems, your failures, your challenges, your barriers, your tragedies, your disappointments, and even your past sins. You need an internal reason to feel better about your external possibilities. Your dream is inside you. It may be dormant, but it is not dead. Think hard and remember.

Now allow that experience, that moment of recollection, to be the springboard that launches you into dreaming again. If you could dream one time, you can dream again. It may not be the same dream, but it may surprise you that a childhood dream was more accurate than you thought—especially if you realize that your dream was a "how" and not a "what."

Think about it. Suppose you dreamed of being president. That dream probably came because of what you thought you could do (and do *better*) if you were president. Even if your chances of becoming president now are zero, your dream of doing something significant on some scale is not far-fetched at all.

When you recall your dream, don't be surprised if, maybe only for a minute, your mind leaves your problems and you take a one-minute break from feeling stuck. Treasure that feeling. It's what is available to you when you pursue your dreams.

I remembered I had dreamed of being a successful public speaker. At the time of my dream, though, I didn't have money to get my car fixed, I couldn't break a habit I thought would kill me one day, and I felt like a complete hypocrite because everyone who knew me thought I had it all together. I had to start over. To do so, I had to dream again.

Once I started to dream again, I started making very short-term plans—like three hours at a time. I didn't project where I would be in three years or one year or six months or even three months. I had to put myself on a plan that projected three hours at a time. Yes—three hours! Someone said that the way you eat an elephant is one bite at a time. I had to rebuild my life one "bite" at a time.

If you are having a problem seeing past your problems, you will have to start by dreaming small dreams and setting goals in three-hour increments. Perhaps you need to open your mail, call three creditors to arrange a new payment plan, call an attorney to review your options, or find two people you can trust with whom you can share your troubles. But do something new—something bold, something proactive, something responsible, something helpful, something positive, something concrete—within the next three hours. Then take another new action during the following three hours.

When you do, you will definitely be on your way to somewhere great by traveling three hours at a time.

Finally, pray. Ask God to give you the strength, the insight, and the good sense to do something meaningful within the next three hours. At the end of three hours, thank Him for allowing you to live and breathe for the previous three hours, realizing that someone didn't make it through those same hours. If you do make it, He allowed you to make it for a reason. Your present test is your future testimony.

God bless you as you begin to dream again.

## ACTION ITEMS

1. List some ways in which you feel stuck.

2. Make a list of new actions you could take to move forward.

3. From the list you just made, do something new every three hours. Then pause and reflect on how you feel.

# PERSONAL GOALS

*When they had crossed, Elijah said to Elisha, "Tell me,*
*what can I do for you before I am taken from you?" "Let me*
*inherit a double portion of your spirit," Elisha replied.*

2 Kings 2:9

Now you are going to zoom in and begin creating or refining your goals. Studies concerning goals have generally come to two conclusions: (1) people with goals achieve more than people without goals, and (2) people with written goals achieve more than those with unwritten goals.[1] The first challenge is to write down your goals if you have not done so already. If you have written your goals, it's time to determine whether they are in their proper position. Most people will never achieve what you will achieve.

_____ cause it's a manageable number. It's cru-
_____ r goals on one side of one piece of paper
_____ gh categories that they describe an entire
_____ time.

*[handwritten note:]*
Study the world
of God, witness
to people,
Relationship Hub
child, Family
work on me
home—

48

If this is all new to you, it will take some time to develop, but congratulations for getting started.

I always begin with personal goals since these goals will determine whether I have what it takes to reach and sustain the others. Of course, all our goals are personal, but what I have learned is that some goals are more personal than others.

The desire for a new job, the need for more money, an interest in new information, and a commitment to more prayer are all personal goals. In fact, the very process I am describing assumes that you set goals that are distinct from the goals of other people, groups, or organizations. In order to maintain your self-esteem, your sense of purpose, and your pursuit of accomplishments, you must have personal goals. It is very difficult, if not impossible, to have healthy relationships with others without having goals for yourself. But it bears repeating that some goals are more personal than others.

Allow me to share with you the personal goals I recently set for myself:

- maintain my current weight
- begin a new daily routine that includes at least one hour of writing
- better manage a key personal relationship

These are examples of what I mean by personal goals. These are areas of my life I can address without help from anyone else. They also represent some "whats" that can be approached in various ways. The "hows" will come later. Personal goals can be one-week, three-month, or one-year goals.

Within the goal-setting process, I distinguish between personal goals and other goals because without such a distinction we can lose sight of some very basic realities. Everyone I know has a type of personal goal—to lose weight, to stop smoking, to work out, to break a bad habit, or something else. These types of goals address our character, our personality, our development as a person, and our humanity. Personal goals in this context are those goals that are for you, about you, and pursued because of the type of person you want to be. Without a specific written commitment with a timetable attached, these types of personal goals are often pushed to the sidelines or the back burner, and they are virtually ignored while you pursue the big-ticket items.

This is why people who are successful in impressive ventures can find themselves undone by some personal flaw that they cannot get under control. Tragically, the people close to such folks can see their personal flaws but they may refuse to confront or assist the person. If you know people whose flaws could destroy them (and those around them), consider how you might speak to them.

When you place your personal goals—your habits, your attitude, and your relationships—alongside your financial and other goals, you give them equal status and equal attention. That's a good thing. These goals are probably so personal that no one else even knows they exist. But when you accomplish them, you know that you have become a better you.

# ACTION ITEMS

1. Identify two or three goals that are so personal you may not be able share them even with people close to you. Write them down.

2. Next to each goal you just identified, create a "by when" timetable. For example, if you wrote down "lose twenty pounds," add something like "by my birthday" or "in a hundred days."

## NOTE

1. "Study Focuses on Strategies for Achieving Goals, Resolutions," Dominican University of California, accessed February 25, 2019, www.dominican .edu/dominicannews/study-highlights-strategies-for-achieving-goals.

## DAY 10

# INTELLECTUAL GOALS

*Do not conform to the pattern of this world, but be transformed*
*by the renewing of your mind. Then you will be able to test and*
*approve what God's will is—his good, pleasing and perfect will.*

Romans 12:2

Now that you have started identifying personal goals, you can proceed to your second category: intellectual goals.

I have earned degrees from three wonderful institutions of higher learning. But the most important knowledge I have acquired was not received in any school. Don't get me wrong—I appreciate my education. I gained significant knowledge from all my schools. But formal education is not the only way to gain knowledge or expand one's intellect.

That perception is one of the barriers to expanding and reaching our intellectual goals. When we consider subject matter we would like to access or even master, we are often discouraged because we have neither the time nor the money to go to school to learn it. But going to college or enrolling in a formal academic program represents a "how" and not a "what." Going to college is *one* way to accomplish an intellectual goal, but it is not the *only* way to get there.

As long as you are alive, you should maintain a list of subjects about which you would like to learn. There may be some language you want to learn to speak, some technology you ___ e to master, some part of history you would like to ___ dish you would like to learn to prepare ___ in your head. If it is, you will di ___ unattained. Rather, you should ___ t of things you want to learn—i ___ ake a commitment to them, you can ___ ng to accomplish the goals.

Today there are nearly unlimi ___ accessible ways to learn. There are free online courses. There are books we can read about everything. There are lectures and workshops we can attend. And there are people who are smart and who love sharing what they know. Even commercial television has some shows that are great sources of knowledge about things that really matter.

There is always an affordable way to gain knowledge on almost any subject. Libraries still lend books for free. I like YouTube; it has videos that cover every subject I have ever needed to know more about. I also have f ___ e courses on every subject taught ___ the world. I have listened to lec ___ out philosophy, history, psychol ___ munications all while walking on ___ ot only am I expanding my intell ___ two separate goals during the same time period—personal and intellectual.

## ACTION ITEMS

1.  Decide what you would like to learn. Write down at least three things.

2.  For each area of knowledge you want to gain, list two or three options you could use to learn about it.

3.  Choose the subject that interests you most and take one action toward learning about it today (watch a YouTube video, buy a book, sign up for a class, etc.).

# DAY 11

---

# VOCATIONAL GOALS

*After this, Paul left Athens and went to Corinth. There he met*
*a Jew named Aquila, a native of Pontus, who had recently come*
*from Italy with his wife Priscilla, because Claudius had ordered*
*all Jews to leave Rome. Paul went to see them, and because he*
*was a tentmaker as they were, he stayed and worked with them.*

Acts 18:1–3

I recently met a woman who gave me two business cards for herself. Before I could ask, the woman's friend offered this explanation: "One card is for the job she has to do, and the other card is for the job she loves to do." I understood exactly what the friend was saying.

There was a time when I was in the exact same situation. I had a job I had to keep in order to pay my bills, but I hated the job. The only good thing about that job was that I received a paycheck every two weeks. However, every day I trudged to my pay-the-bills job, I knew what my dream job was. I finally made up my mind to pursue my real career and get paid for doing what I love to do.

That is what it takes to set career goals. It involves describing your life's real work and not settling for a job just to pay the bills. The first question to ask yourself is, What kind of work would you do if you did not need money? What do you love doing so much that you would do it without any compensation? Most of us would initially say that we would do anything for the right amount of money, but that may not be true. I recently told a professional athlete that he did not seem to be happy playing his sport. Many well-paid people are miserable, while many low-wage earners love what they do.

I have a friend who loves cleaning cars. He takes pride in it—he longs to do it—and he will come to your house if a car is there for him to clean. As a result of his love for this work, he cleans cars better than anyone I have ever met. That is because we do best what we most love to do.

So that is another question you must answer before settling into a vocation or profession: What do you love to do more than anything else in the world? There is no guarantee that you will get a job right away doing what you love. You are more likely to find or create a job that you love after you identify what that is and then spend some time doing it somewhere—even if only in a volunteer role at first.

You must also be able to identify what you do so well that someone would be willing to pay you to do it. My sister-in-law organizes offices and paperwork so well that people are willing to pay her to do it. My friend who cleans cars can earn hundreds of dollars every day. Our economy is based on supply and demand. If you know what you can supply, finding out where it is needed is the key to your employment.

So when developing your vocational goals, you should build on your passions, stay in touch with your dreams, and do what you must until you can do what you love. The questions below will help you shape your career goals.

## ACTION ITEMS

1.  List one task you love doing so much that you would do it without being paid. What is your dream job?

2.  What things do you do so well that people would be willing to pay you to do them?

3.  What is the most important step you must take to get closer to your dream job?

---

# FINANCIAL GOALS (PART 1)

*If you have not been trustworthy in handling worldly
wealth, who will trust you with true riches?*

Luke 16:11

Too many of us are in survival mode when it comes to our finances. I hear so many people describing their desire to simply hold on to what they have or saying that they're just trying to make ends meet. That is exactly how I used to live. In fact, I was even worse. I was paying last month's bills with next week's check and dodging bill collectors. One day I decided I was not going to live that way for the rest of my life. I had to set some financial goals in order to develop a financial strategy.

Most of us will need help in establishing our financial goals. We all have dreams, and there are financial implications attached to our dreams. But a goal is much more concrete than a dream. A goal is something that is achievable through the execution of a reasonable plan. I can dream of buying a castle, but when I set that as my goal,

I'd better be able to explain how I am going to do that. It helps to have a certified financial planner work with us in developing our financial goals. However, even before you solicit the help of professionals, there are some things you can do for yourself.

In *Say Yes to No Debt*, I outlined four levels for achieving financial freedom. The first step is to "Get Started." That means it is important to stop dreaming and start planning, to stop talking and start taking action to change our financial status. To begin, we must undertake two important tasks.

First, keep a record of all the money you spend in a thirty-day period. At the end of those thirty days, take a look at the list of expenditures and circle the ones that are not absolutely necessary for your survival. All the circled items represent money that you can use to help you reach your financial goals.

Next, obtain a copy of your credit report. You can obtain free copies of your credit report once a year from AnnualCreditReport .com, and your inquiry does not affect your credit score. There are three main credit reporting agencies that contribute to your credit score.

I actually get my report from each of the three credit bureaus— Equifax, TransUnion, and Experian—once a year, but I get a report every four months from one of them. By staggering my requests, I am able to keep up with what's happening with my credit all year long and at no cost. Our credit reports reveal not only our credit history but also information about our credit and our identity in general. Identity theft is a growing problem, and our credit reports often inform us about unauthorized attempts to use our personal information.

Financial goals describe where you would like to be financially by a certain date. Obviously the shorter the interval between now and your target date, the smaller the goals.

But financial goals are more than numbers; they also reflect your values. God wants you to use your money for a purpose. Some purposes have more value than others. After you make sure your basic needs are covered, the way you use your money and the purposes for which you accumulate money reflect the kind of person you are and the kind of legacy you will leave.

My grandmother was born in 1901, and when she died in 1981, she owned multiple homes that were all debt free. She left an inheritance for her children and grandchildren. My goal is to do at least as well as she did.

It does not matter how much money you currently earn. You can begin the process of building your financial future by properly managing your financial present.

## ACTION ITEMS

1. Estimate how much you spend in an average week on basic living expenses.

2. For the next two weeks, compare your actual spending with your estimated spending.

3. Obtain a copy of your credit report at AnnualCreditReport.com.

DAY 13

# FINANCIAL GOALS (PART 2)

*The borrower is slave to the lender.*

Proverbs 22:7

You will never get ahead financially until you get out of debt. Debt erodes your ability to save. Debt eliminates your ability to accumulate wealth. Debt can lower your credit score and make it harder to access capital for investment. The Bible even equates debt with slavery (see Prov. 22:7)!

I learned this the hard way. I was one of those people who assumed debt was normal and acceptable. That assumption changed one day when I heard a preacher say that we should purchase our cars with cash. I thought the man was drunk! As I sat and listened to him, he explained that we were paying more than we should for our cars when we add the interest payments to the principal payments. I did the math and realized that on a three-year car note, I was paying $2,562.18 in interest on a $20,000 car loan! And that was with an 8 percent interest rate. Some people are paying as much as 28 percent interest on auto loans, paying nearly $30,000 on a $20,000 loan over three years!

More important than the money I was spending was the fact that I had never given it a moment of thought. I felt utterly ordinary doing what I was doing. And unfortunately, I was normal. Americans use borrowing as a means of purchasing cars and almost everything else. While that is great for the banks and the finance companies, it eats away at our financial capacity. And we feel as if we have no choice. I realized I did have options and I had to change my attitude about money.

That is what I am asking you to do. Change your attitude about money, starting with debt.

Of course, no one will become debt free in a day or two. But if your approach is that it is preferable to be free of all debt, then your goals and decisions will reflect that attitude. You will stop charging items on your credit cards that will take years to pay off. You will not feel as if you need a new car as soon as you make your last payment on the old car. You will treat debt as a temporary condition and indeed devise a strategy to get out of debt.

Not everyone is as I used to be. Not all of us spend our way into debt. Some people are in debt because of medical expenses, prolonged unemployment, divorce, student loans, or something else. It doesn't matter how you got into debt. What matters is how you plan to get out of debt. The challenge is to hate debt so much that you make getting out of debt your priority.

When you are debt free, you can open businesses, invest money, donate generously, and live a stress-free life. Debt should be a strategy not a lifestyle. Planning to be debt free is the next step as you establish your financial goals.

## ACTION ITEMS

1.  Make a list of all your debts, from the smallest to the largest.

2.  Set a date when you would like to be debt free.

3.  Visit BillionDollarPayDown.com and explore some ways to manage your personal debt reduction strategy.

# FINANCIAL GOALS (PART 3)

*A good person leaves an inheritance for their children's children.*

Proverbs 13:22

Setting financial goals can be a difficult task. The cost of living is high. Sometimes it seems as if you have little control over your income. For many of us the only financial goal we have is just to survive. So how do some people seem to break out of survival mode and make a good living?

Having financial goals does not guarantee that you will be prosperous. But not having financial goals makes it almost certain that you will be on a financial treadmill for the rest of your life—moving but going nowhere.

I have never taken any formal courses in finance, budgeting, business, or investing. Most of what I have learned has come from failure. But I discovered that it is never too late to get started with financial planning.

Like with your other goals, there are two fundamental ways to set financial goals. You can start with those small steps that you can take immediately (example: saving one dollar a week), or you can start by projecting where you would like to be in three years (example: $3,000 saved).

In the first approach, the savings goal grows out of the small steps you plan to take—saving one dollar a week. That means you will have saved fifty-two dollars in a year ($1.00 x 52 weeks). If that amount of savings does not satisfy you, then try $1.50 or $2.00 per week. The objective is to have a concrete goal that is attainable.

The second approach is one that will "back you into" a plan. A goal to save $3,000 in three years means that you will have to save an average of $19.23 every week ($3,000/156 weeks). If you can save that much every week, then your goal is realistic. If you can save more, you can increase your goal or reach your goal sooner.

This level of specificity and planning is how you take control of your finances and your life. Some people call this intentional living. Once you start living this way, you will find that goals become clearer and much more attainable.

It is tempting to immerse yourself in economic analysis, reciting the evils of past injustices, lamenting the unfairness of various aspects of the economy, and brooding over the challenges you face today. It is sometimes fun to wallow in those thoughts, and sometimes I did. But I found that at the end of those exercises, I still had to pay my rent and handle my other responsibilities. And I was depressed and weighed down by the challenges I had just reminded myself of. So I chose taking action over spouting philosophy, and the results in my life have been rewarding.

I urge you to do the same. Sure, you must understand the systems that surround and influence you. But analysis and understanding do not pay the bills—unless you are a professor paid to teach ideas! You need a financial strategy that is built on financial goals that you must set for yourself.

## ACTION ITEMS

1. Set your debt reduction goals. Either write out two or three small steps you'll take, or write down where you'd like to be in three years.

2. Set a goal to save up an emergency fund of at least $3,000 in cash. Write down how much you'll save each week or month and when you'll reach this goal.

DAY 15

# SPIRITUAL GOALS

*What good will it be for someone to gain the*
*whole world, yet forfeit their soul?*

Matthew 16:26

When considering spiritual goals, it is essential to begin by distinguishing between something that is religious and something that is spiritual. *Religion* is the system that you embrace in pursuit of or in response to your beliefs. *Spirit* is that intangible, internal reality that is the essence of who you are as a human.

You should never forget that you are not a body that happens to have a spirit inside. Instead, you are a spirit that happens to have an earthly body that you wear for a few years. That is why your spirit affects your body much more than your body affects your spirit. When your spirit is low or weak, your physical capacity is diminished and you are vulnerable to physical ailments. But when your body is fragile, it is entirely possible to have a healthy and vibrant spirit.

You need to set goals for your spiritual strength and capacity to undergird and complement the other areas of your life. Your fears, stresses, hopes, self-esteem, patience, vision, temperament, joys, and sorrows are all examples of areas of your life related to your spirit.

*[handwritten margin note: Mind/ Intellect emotions & will (Heart)]*

Your religious life should enhance your spiritual life and contribute to the development of your spiritual strength. But everyone—regardless of religious views—has a spirit. A spirit lives for eternity after the body has ceased to function, but a body without a spirit is a corpse. When you get to heaven, your spirit will get a new body. You should not neglect your spirit.

There are many ways to build on one's spiritual foundation. Your spiritual goals should describe what kind of spiritual character you would like to possess.

In many ways, your spiritual "what" comes very close to your spiritual "how." This is different from the other categories of your life. For instance, you may have a spiritual goal to be a more prayerful person. Prayer is the means by which humans remain in contact with the Divine. The benefits of prayer include securing more certainty about life's purpose, approaching decisions with divine assistance, maintaining a greater sense of humility and possibility by remaining connected to divine power, and submitting to divine will rather than pursuing only one's own desires. These are all valuable "whats" to desire.

But what is interesting about the spiritual goal of prayer is that the "how" to reach the "what" includes prayer itself. There are things you can do to become more prayerful—like reading books about prayer, listening to talks about prayer, and hearing the prayers of others. But the way to become a more prayerful person necessarily requires participating in prayer itself.

If your goal is to have more money, you cannot reach it only by deciding to have more money. But if you want a more prayerful life, you can get there merely by including more prayer in your life.

Setting spiritual goals will make the difference between a life with temporary success and a life with lasting quality. It was Jesus who said that it does not matter if you gain the world but lose your soul (see Matt. 16:26).

## ACTION ITEMS

1. Name three spiritual goals you will pursue.

    1, Closer relationship w/ God
    2.) Witnesses
    3) Read/Know the Bible
       and to give to other in
       A common why

2. Describe how your life will be better as a result of achieving those goals.

    1. Deal with Pursuit Matter
    2.) Be Patient w/ People
    3.

3. Identify someone you believe has attained each goal you seek and find out how that person became who he or she is.

# FINE-TUNING GOALS

*This is what the LORD Almighty says: "Give
careful thought to your ways."*

Haggai 1:7

You are halfway through the thirty-one-day makeover! You may be amazed at how much you have already accomplished. You may be amazed at how fast the time is flying by.

It helps me to think in terms of what's actually so. No matter how these two weeks have felt or how things seem, the simple reality is that you are two weeks older. And here's another reality: your behavior during the last two weeks has determined your status today.

That is how life works. Either you die or you keep on living. And you are alive—hopefully doing some new things, thinking some new thoughts, and pursuing some new dreams. The major accomplishment so far should be a new appreciation for goals.

Before I begin to describe how to manage the process of reaching goals, I want you to review what you have done thus far and spend some time analyzing the results.

I have stated that you are much more successful when you have written goals. I have also said that your written goals should be divided into five categories to have a snapshot of a complete life—personal, intellectual, vocational, financial, and spiritual. I have spent the last several days offering brief descriptions and examples for these categories. Your objective is to write down two or three specific items under each category to flesh out the outline of your goals.

This strategy requires that you fit all this information on one side of one sheet of letter-sized paper. Whether you are planning for three weeks, three months, or three years, there is value in being able to see your entire life on one side of one sheet of paper. When you do that, you can look at your goals in proximity to one another and analyze their potential impact on one another. This is vital.

It is critical to remember that great goals can conflict with one another if you are not careful to consider the goals as a whole. A friend once shared with me that she had the goals of paying off all her debt, going back to college as a full-time student, and quitting her job to have time for school. These were all great goals, but it was not feasible for her to quit her job and pay all her bills too. She hadn't considered the conflict that existed between those admirable goals. In her attempt to create a plan for success, she had created a plan for failure.

This happens much more than you might imagine. Good people with meaningful goals fail to consider them as a whole and end up accomplishing very little without ever realizing why.

Write down your goals. If you have never done this before, I suggest that you start by focusing on just the next few weeks or months. After you analyze the goals you have written, you may discover a need to modify a particular goal because of its impact on another goal. Then you will be ready to develop a strategy for accomplishing your goals.

## ACTION ITEMS

1.  Use your goal chart (found in the appendix) to write down your goals. Focus on planning for the upcoming weeks and months.

2.  Review the goals you have written and make any necessary modifications. You may need to modify your goals because of other goals you have, time constraints, things that have to happen first, or other conflicts. Make sure your goals are not conflicting.

—

# IT'S ABOUT TIME

*Be on guard! Be alert! You do not know when that time will come.*

Mark 13:33

These three statements people make about time drive me crazy:

- "I don't know where the time goes."
- "If I just had more time …"
- "I try to manage my time."

Let's consider each of these statements.

First, time goes where time has always gone—into the past. The truth is that all of us do know where time goes. When we make that statement, we mean that time is moving forward while we seem to be standing still. It seems as if my twin sons turned eighteen years old in under eighteen years. But when they did turn eighteen, I was not surprised. They had been seventeen years old for the previous twelve months! People who find themselves making this statement about time will also find themselves accomplishing less than they could have in the time they do have.

Second, you are not going to get any more time. Period. It is a ridiculous statement and one worth deleting from our verbal repertoire. The implication is that you would do something great or achieve greater success if you had more time. The key to winning is figuring out how to best use the time you *have*. Wishing for more time is a waste of time.

Third, you cannot manage time. Time does not stand still—its linear progression is a fixed reality—and time belongs to God. The idea of time management sounds catchy and cute, but you cannot manage time. You manage your *life*, and you use time in the process. I have learned to look at time as one of my most precious commodities. Before I owned any securities, before I owned any real estate, before I had any financial capacity, I realized that I was a wealthy person because I had a considerable supply of time. I would rather waste money than waste time. You can always get more money, but you can never get more time.

So rather than lamenting how quickly time moves or wishing for more of it, the most productive response is to develop a strategic use of the time you do have. I recommend making a chart that divides the week into one-hour blocks. The purpose of this chart is to fill in the blocks of time that you do regularly scheduled activities. (You can exclude the hours that you usually are sleeping.) After you fill in the activities you usually do, you will see empty boxes. These are the times you can begin to fill with activities that will help you reach your goals.

The only way to accomplish your goals is to invest sufficient time in pursuing them.

# ACTION ITEMS

1. Estimate how many hours you spend per week doing your various activities. What is the total?

2. Make copies of the weekly one-hour block chart (found in the appendix) and fill one out for the upcoming week. Then compare the actual hours with your original estimate.

3. Identify how much time you are spending on activities directly related to your goals. How much time do you spend on unrelated activities?

DAY 18

——

# SETTING PRIORITIES

*Seek first his kingdom and his righteousness, and*
*all these things will be given to you as well.*

Matthew 6:33

I don't think I have ever had only one important responsibility to manage. Not only has my entire adult life been an exciting journey of interesting projects and stimulating positions, but I have also found myself having multiple responsibilities and roles co-occurring. As a result, I have had to answer one question perhaps more than any other: "How do you wear so many different hats?"

The idea of wearing different hats always conjures in my mind the notion that I somehow have different personalities or identities. But I have always worked hard to be the same person in every role. I answer like this: "I only have one head, so I can only wear one hat!"

I never considered the challenge to be the wearing of different hats. Instead, I always believed that the task has been to wear the same hat in different places. Your priority should be to remain unashamedly authentic in every environment. Once you start changing hats, I am afraid you will get caught being one type of person in one place and a different kind of person in other places.

The question is sometimes put like this: "How do you balance all your roles?" That's a fair question. It seeks to probe more deeply into the process of handling multiple roles with integrity. One need not be in multiple public roles to have this challenge. We all have various tasks, purposes, and goals to juggle. Therefore, we need a process for effectively managing those tasks and roles.

The key word for developing this process is *priorities*. If you have a systematic way of determining your priorities, you will be able to follow Stephen Covey's advice in his book *7 Habits of Highly Effective People* and spend most of your time working on matters that are important but not urgent.[1]

I discovered that, without thinking about it, I had developed an excellent process for setting priorities. I call it the bracket process—like bracketology for NCAA playoffs. This approach pits priorities against each other like teams on the road to the Final Four in college basketball. The winners of the first round go on to play other winners of the first round, and then the winners of those contests play each other too, and so on, until one priority beats out all the others and becomes the thing I do next.

When you have multiple roles, you have multiple activities competing for your time and attention. Before you begin, if you place your list of tasks into brackets, you can see which one wins over the others by determining which is most important. If you do this in writing, it does not take more than a few minutes to have a written list of things to do with their ranking in the order of importance.

You can then assign time to each task as needed and experience stress-free pursuit of multiple goals. And you will need only one hat!

## ACTION ITEMS

1. Use or adapt the priorities bracket (found in the appendix) to determine what your top priorities are for the rest of this month.

2. Schedule all your top priorities on your calendar as if they are important meetings. Remember to celebrate when you get them done!

## NOTE

1. Stephen R. Covey, *The 7 Habits of Highly Effective People: Powerful Lessons in Personal Change* (New York: Simon & Schuster, 2013), 162.

DAY 19

# ARE YOUR GOALS BIG ENOUGH?

*To him who is able to do immeasurably more than*
*all we ask or imagine, according to his power that*
*is at work within us, to him be glory.*

Ephesians 3:20–21

Imagine that you have achieved all your thirty-one-day goals during the first eighteen days of the month. Wow! What a blessing! And what a surprise! You had some pretty big goals in some very critical areas of your life.

Don't worry if you haven't gotten them all done yet. It's a thirty-one-day challenge, after all, not an eighteen-day challenge. But take a minute to acknowledge the progress you have made.

Also take time to acknowledge those who have helped or encouraged you on your way. The feedback I have received from so many people when we have walked through these thirty-one-day journeys together has been such an encouragement. I have felt their love, appreciation, and support. It is true that "two are better than one" (Eccl. 4:9). It is much easier to reach challenging objectives when you know you are not walking alone.

The completion of your goal chart and your time chart has been our focus for the past few days. I hope you have taken those tasks seriously. I also hope you were able to identify and list your priorities.

My passion is to help people with their financial lives. But as I have stated, it is vital to approach any part of your life by addressing your entire life. People who are sloppy with handling their money are usually careless in other areas of their lives too. Gaining control of your life is the prerequisite for obtaining control of your finances.

The rest of this journey will assume that you have concrete goals in the five critical areas of your life. Take the time to do that right now if you have not already done so. And if you have, please review your goals and be sure they are big enough to meet your needs.

After today there are twelve days left in our thirty-one-day makeover. While there is no magic attached to day 31, it is essential to set goals, create deadlines, and celebrate small victories. This one-month exercise is only a step into a future of building long-term plans. But you have to begin somewhere.

What do you do if you find yourself achieving your goals ahead of schedule? First, celebrate! Thank God for the strength and the victory! Next, you must assess your goals and make sure they were big enough. It doesn't help to set goals that are too small. But in either case, it is time to set new goals. I may rest and celebrate for a day, but there is still more to do.

## ACTION ITEMS

1. If you have achieved your goals ahead of schedule, celebrate! Do something special for yourself.

2. Make a list of things you could do to celebrate once you have achieved all your goals for the month.

3. Assess your goals. Are they too big or too small? What adjustments do you need to make with twelve days left in this makeover challenge?

# CONTROL WHAT YOU CAN CONTROL

*For lack of discipline they will die, led
astray by their own great folly.*

Proverbs 5:23

It is incredible how much progress you can make if you begin to focus on yourself and create written goals that you are committed to reaching.

Of course, there are certain events and circumstances in your life that cannot be controlled. But if you take control of those things that you can control, you will be in a better position to find your way through those things you cannot control.

When I was diagnosed with prostate cancer, it was a very intimidating moment. However, because I had changed my lifestyle at the beginning of that same year—walking at least four miles every morning, drinking plenty of water, eliminating the consumption of sweets—I was able to anticipate and experience a complete and speedy recovery after my surgery.

I often find that the problems I can't avoid are made worse by having failed to prevent the issues I could've prevented. This discovery has been so liberating for me.

When you read that, does something pop into your mind? I think of someone I know who tends to think in terms of victimhood. When a serious health matter befell that person, it was made so much worse by a negative mentality. I wonder how much better his life would be and whether his health would have been able to spring back quickly if he had instead developed a positive and empowered and hopeful and prayerful approach to life.

What situations in your life do you know you need to work on now so that if something negative happens, it won't set off an avalanche of (preventable) problems? This preparatory work needs to show up in your goals.

At the end of our makeover, you will be in a certain condition. What do you want that to be? One way to have a vision for the outcome is to answer this question: "Who will I see—or who will others see—when they look at me?" The more you ask and answer this question, the more likely it is that you are making the most out of your life.

For some people this discussion is uncomfortable because it feels as if this process places too much emphasis on individual needs and wants. Many people are uneasy hearing and thinking about themselves as much as I suggest. But the reality is that you are not in a position to help others if you have not addressed your own needs and potential.

On every airline flight I have taken, I have been instructed that in the case of an emergency I should place the oxygen mask on myself before I attempt to help anyone else. The sense behind that advice is this: if you are not all right, you will not be able to help other passengers make it to safety.

## ACTION ITEMS

1. What issues do you know you need to address that would make matters much worse if something big goes wrong?

2. It is now day 20. Who will you see in the mirror twelve days from now?

# LIVE OUTSIDE THE BOX

*The Spirit God gave us does not make us timid,*
*but gives us power, love and self-discipline.*

2 Timothy 1:7

One result of having goals that are too small is that you lower your standards. If your whole goal for today is sitting up in bed, you're not going to achieve much more than that. The key to winning the battle against mediocre and unproductive living is a commitment to living outside the boxes in which you find yourself. And there are plenty of boxes to consider.

One of the most important boxes keeping you stuck on small goals is that of others' expectations. What people around you expect you to do, what you think you are supposed to do, what the culture says you should do … can all easily become self-imposed pressures that can kill you! The forces of cultural, social, and even so-called religious expectations are so strong that you can forfeit your individuality and your right to choose without even knowing it.

I am not an advocate of abandoning tradition just for the sake of novelty. Nor do I condone thumbing our noses at beliefs that have sustained us through the years. But it is essential for you to carve out your strategies and not let cultural groupthink become a substitute for your responsibility to make independent choices.

Christians often find themselves standing against their surrounding culture. You may have to reject the newest and most popular trends or lifestyles in order to realize your potential and accomplish your goals. Too many people live within boundaries set for them by others rather than setting their sights on their own beliefs and goals. Only God's boundaries should matter.

Another box you may have to climb out of is your family box. When young David was preparing to slay Goliath, it was his oldest brother, Eliab, who tried to discourage him from going forward (see 1 Sam. 17:28). David's brother saw him only as a little shepherd boy. He did not see him as a giant killer.

Because your family members know you best, they can be the very people who see no future for you beyond the past they know. If you let them, they will keep you in their little boxes, and you will never outgrow their perceptions of you. To be the person you desire to be, you may have to break out of a few family molds. It was a good thing David refused to stay in his family box. All Jewish history might have been different had he remained in the box. He never would have slain Goliath.

Perhaps the most challenging box to escape is the box of your fears. Whether it is the fear of speaking in public, the fear of making a commitment, or the fear of personal failure, all of us have fears. The only way to overcome a fear is to confront and engage it. Fear cannot be thought away, prayed away, smiled away, cried away, or wished away. You must force yourself to do that which you fear until you no longer fear it. Otherwise, you will live in the box of fear for the rest of your life.

Your boxes are only as strong as you allow them to be. Are you going to allow some box or someone's view of you to keep you from being the person you desire to be? You have the power to be that person. But it will require a little box bursting.

## ACTION ITEMS

1.  What cultural or social box has the potential to undermine your success?

2. Identify a family box you need to break out of or you have to be careful to avoid.

3. What fear do you need to overcome?

# DON'T GET TRICKED INTO GIVING UP

*Do not be deceived: God cannot be mocked.*
*A man reaps what he sows.*

Galatians 6:7

Most of us have difficulty completely embracing motivational messages. Despite the popularity of many bestselling motivational books and the success of many well-paid motivational speakers, most of us have not found the success they promised. The evidence of so much failure around us undermines our belief in the positive and motivating messages we hear. Too often a great speech, a great book, or just a motivational moment functions like a meal, soon after which you find yourself hungry again.

Every time I've led a thirty-one-day makeover, all the participants were excited about starting. But then inevitably some would drop out, others would lose interest, others would become distracted, and a few would even just give up on the possibility of being somewhere new by day 31.

How does that happen? What causes us to be totally committed to something one minute and abandon our commitment just a few days (or minutes) later? What makes us cool down so quickly after having such passion for a particular pursuit?

I have found that this happens for one of two reasons. We never truly committed in the first place, or somewhere along the way we were tricked into believing that what we desired was either not possible or no longer desirable.

I used the word *tricked* purposefully. We have been programmed to believe that *opposition* is the greatest threat to success. But opposition is actually what makes you stronger, superior, and successful. True greatness excels over opposition. Without opposition, there is no way to know that greatness exists.

No, it is *deception* that undermines your dreams and your destiny. When you are deceived, you become convinced that your goals are unattainable because of some circumstance or occurrence or false belief. When you are deceived, you become convinced that there is something better than your goals or that you should abandon them now to save face.

That is why it is so important to write your goals, meditate on your goals, pray about your goals, and budget your time in pursuit of your goals. It is so tempting to allow distractions, discouragement, or derailment to deceive you into concluding that your goals are not worth the trouble or are out of reach. Every great person I have ever studied had to press through obstacles and endure some degree of hardship to stay focused on his or her goals.

Babe Ruth was both the home-run king and the strikeout king. He missed the ball more than anyone else, and that could've made him give up. But he kept swinging at the ball! He didn't give up.

If LeBron James had allowed his missed baskets to convince him that he should forget about basketball, he would not have become a superstar and MVP. If Helen Keller had allowed her deafness and blindness to convince her that she was not important, she would not have become the first deaf and blind person to earn a bachelor of arts degree. If Nelson Mandela had allowed his incarceration to convince him to give up, he never would have become president of South Africa after spending twenty-seven years in jail.

These are but a few examples of people who were not deceived by their circumstances or defeated by their failures. All of them knew what they wanted and were determined to let nothing permanently stand in their way.

So don't be deceived or discouraged. You have the right and the potential to reach your goals. It's time for you to really "do you"!

## ACTION ITEMS

1. What obstacles have you faced while working to accomplish your goals? List those obstacles below.

2. Now rewrite the obstacles from your list above as opportunities for reaching your goals. (Example: Being sick for a few days this month took some time away from pursuing my goals, but making up for that lost time led me to new time-management strategies.) Turn the obstacles into opportunities.

# FRIENDS MATTER

*A friend loves at all times, and a brother*
*is born for a time of adversity.*

Proverbs 17:17

When I first joined Facebook, I found it interesting that the designation for contacts is "friends." The more people became my so-called friends on Facebook, the sillier I felt having so many people who were willing to call themselves my friends. When my number of Facebook friends reached five thousand, I received a message from Facebook telling me I could not have any new friends unless I deleted some of my old friends.

Initially this was a challenge. *What would people think*, I wondered, *when they realized I had deleted them?* But after I reviewed many of the names on my list of Facebook friends, I realized that I really did not know many of them personally. In fact, after more careful observation, it appeared that many of these folks not only were unknown to me but also had postings and profiles that suggested I may not want to know them at all. So deleting certain Facebook friends did not pose a problem.

Then I realized there were people in my actual life—not my social media life—whom I did know but whom I should probably consider deleting as friends also. It is very hard to pursue goals while maintaining friendships with people who have no interest in the goals you are working toward. Instead, you should actively seek relationships with people who are attempting to accomplish goals similar to yours. Loyalty to certain friends can undermine your successes and accomplishments.

If you are trying to change, you are always better off having a few good friends who appreciate and support your efforts rather than hundreds of so-called friends who are doing the exact opposite of what you are trying to do. It is so much easier to exercise, lose weight, stop gambling, read books, worship God, get out of debt, invest money, and generally improve your life when you are striving toward those goals alongside other people.

You should not wait for others to join you before you get started. But you should realize the value of having others on your team. I have learned that it is very helpful to share my goals with a short list of real friends and ask them to support my efforts in some way. Carefully chosen people who partner with you in pursuit of your goals can be more valuable than money.

# ACTION ITEMS

1. Whom do you want on your team? Make your list of people and then recruit your team!

2. Who are some "friends" you need to let drop from your life because they're not pursuing similar goals to your own?

   I do not share goals

# A REAL FRIEND

*A man that hath friends must shew himself friendly: and*
*there is a friend that sticketh closer than a brother.*

Proverbs 18:24 KJV

Friends come and friends go, but a true friend sticks by you like family. Once we concede that we do need friends, this proverb warns us that in order to make and keep friends, we must ourselves be friendly. It is so easy to ignore your responsibility in friendship and simply focus on the benefits. But if everyone wants a friend and no one is committed to being a friend, then we have a serious problem.

For the past few years, I have maintained a personal goal of being a better friend to some specific people. I am embarrassed about how long it took to make this a priority. But I have been blessed with so many friends—and I mean really good friends. There came a time when I had to assess whether anyone considered me as good a friend as I considered so many.

In my commitment to become a real friend, I learned

- a real friend checks on a friend just to see how she is doing.
- a real friend encourages a friend who is not doing so well.
- a real friend sticks close to a friend who is in deep trouble.
- a real friend tells a friend the truth in love.
- a real friend supports a friend when it is no longer popular to do so.
- a real friend makes it easy for a friend to help him.
- a real friend does not put a friend in jeopardy.
- a real friend takes advice as well as she gives advice.
- a real friend prays for his friend.
- a real friend is as happy for a friend's success as she would be for her own.
- a real friend hurts just as much when a friend is in pain as he would if he were in pain.
- a real friend helps a friend reach goals.
- a real friend is hard to find and harder to be.

Don't stop with finding good friends. Work hard to *be* a real friend.

## ACTION ITEMS

1. Friendships can be an integral part of achieving our goals. List five characteristics you admire in your close friends.

2. List five characteristics you will commit to exercising that will help *you* be a better friend.

# PLAN TO DO NOTHING

*Because so many people were coming and going that they did not even have a chance to eat, [Jesus] said to them, "Come with me by yourselves to a quiet place and get some rest."*

Mark 6:31

The idea you must use time effectively and have a plan that accounts for every minute of every day does not mean you are always busy with tasks. Many people who see me from a distance or who receive my advice about linking time to goals assume I advocate perpetual activity. But those who know me well know that while I am a firm believer in planning the use of every hour of the day, that includes planning to do nothing.

Gordon MacDonald wrote a book some years ago entitled *Ordering Your Private World* in which he made a distinction between being called and being driven.[1] That distinction helped me understand that it is not healthy to pursue even laudable goals in a way that ignores personal needs, relational responsibilities, and the importance of being reflective. This is what he called being driven.

Many people are so driven to reach goals and attain success that they ruin their own lives and destroy the lives of those close to them. The alternative understanding offered in the book is that we are all called to a purpose and that our calling should embrace self-nurture.[2] Passionate pursuit of an all-consuming mission need not conflict with personal growth and reflection.

When you develop your time charts or personal schedules, the key is to actually schedule time for self-care. If you use every minute of every day for tasks, you leave no time for thoughts or plans about those tasks. If you are completely consumed with helping others, you run the risk of doing too little for yourself. Even Jesus often withdrew by Himself to pray and be alone (see Luke 5:16).

If you were to look at my schedule, you would notice three types of "do nothing" times. The first is time to do nothing significant pertaining to my work. This is time when I watch movies, read books or magazines, or participate in some leisure or recreational activity that has nothing to do with my work. These activities give me a mental break.

The second is time when I do nothing physical, but I spend time reflecting and planning my work. This is time when I make plans for the church, my businesses, my family, or myself. During this time, I appear to be doing nothing, but I am really doing nothing that others want me to do. I'm not responding to their needs during these times. In my business there is always something I could be doing to help someone else, so I have to schedule time to not do that.

The third "do nothing" time is spent doing literally nothing at all. Some might call this meditation, and sometimes it is. But during this time, I rest my mind and my body without going to sleep. And all these times are written onto my schedule so it doesn't look as if these times are available for doing something else. In that sense I am doing something by doing nothing.

Committing to such times will help protect you from undermining the truly important aspects of your life. It will keep you from passionately pursuing great goals while ignoring your basic needs. You have to find a sustainable way of working, and self-care is a big part of sustainability.

## ACTION ITEMS

1. Pay attention to what you have marked on your schedule. Have you planned time for rest?

2. How would you like to spend your rest time (reading, journaling, listening to music, etc.)?

## NOTES

1. Gordon MacDonald, *Ordering Your Private World*, rev. ed. (Nashville: Thomas Nelson, 1985), 29–37, 140–42.

2. MacDonald, *Ordering Your Private World*, 55–56, 161–75.

# PERSONAL MISSION STATEMENT

*I press on toward the goal to win the prize for which*
*God has called me heavenward in Christ Jesus.*

Philippians 3:14

Every great company or organization has a mission statement. This is a brief statement—usually no more than a few sentences—that describes its purpose for existing and what it seeks to accomplish. This statement functions as a guide for all corporate or organizational activities and explains why any particular task is being performed.

A few years ago, I started a foundation to carry out my mission of helping people with their finances. The name of the foundation is the dfree Global Foundation, Inc. This is the mission statement: "To empower underserved communities by providing resources that help individuals and families achieve financial freedom and self-sufficiency."

Every activity that the foundation undertakes can be explained by the manner in which it aligns with that mission. There are some wonderful opportunities to engage in work that helps people but does not contribute to that mission. In such instances the foundation is obliged to decline offers to be involved.

The best advice I ever received was to write a mission statement for my life. It is fine to have goals that commit your life to certain outcomes by certain dates. But those goals exist within the context of your life's mission. Creating a life mission statement is not as easy as it sounds. And the exact words may be amended or refined as the years pass. But being able to describe your life's mission in a few words can be one of the greatest accomplishments you ever achieve.

You have already written your mission (see day 4). Now it's time to make sure it is still your mission statement.

## ACTION ITEMS

1.  Review and revise your personal mission statement from day 4.

2.  What has changed since day 4, and why?

# STUFF HAPPENS

*In this world you will have trouble. But take
heart! I have overcome the world.*

John 16:33

I had spent an entire week in California, and for some reason I had earthquakes on my mind throughout the trip. The thought of experiencing an earthquake is quite intimidating. I remember when we had a mild earthquake in New Jersey. Someone tweeted that he had moved to the East Coast from the West Coast precisely to get away from earthquakes. Then there was an earthquake on the East Coast!

That is how life unfolds. Stuff just happens. And the point of remembering that fact is to factor the unexpected into your plans. This has been a sobering lesson for me. If I allow myself just enough time to get to my meeting, I have left no room for traffic on the road. If I am not careful when going to the airport to catch a flight, I will not leave enough time for long security lines. If I do not properly insure myself, I will not be prepared for accidents or other occurrences. If I spend every dime I earn, I will have saved nothing for a rainy day or a jobless season.

It is not likely that many of us were prepared for an earthquake on the East Coast. After all, before the 2011 earthquake in Virginia, the last eastern earthquake of that magnitude was in 1897. So we can excuse ourselves for not having had earthquake insurance. But the same cannot be said about apartment insurance, long-term disability insurance, and certainly not life insurance. Earthquakes may come every one hundred years, but death happens every day. The no of death should not stop you from making preparations for what happens after you die.

What if your plans are undermined by events beyond your control? Are you prepared for the unexpected? I have learned to expect the unexpected by hoping and praying for the best but planning and preparing for the worst. You cannot control what happens, but you can control how you respond ... if you are prepared.

In my book *dfree Lifestyle: 12 Steps to Financial Freedom*, I have included a fairly comprehensive discussion about preparing for things that can happen in an effort to "minimize the stress" in our lives. Being prepared for the stuff that may happen makes it easier to pursue those things you want to happen.

# ACTION ITEMS

1. How have you prepared for life's emergencies? List the preparations you have already made below.

2. How can you protect yourself and your assets in the event of an emergency? List steps to prepare yourself for unexpected events.

# MAKE FAILURE WORK FOR YOU

*Though the righteous fall seven times, they rise again,*
*but the wicked stumble when calamity strikes.*

Proverbs 24:16

Failure is inevitable for those who attempt to do something. Some believe it makes no sense to create goals or make plans because they are intimidated by the possibility of failure. Others have experienced so many failures they assume they will always fail at whatever they try. But properly understood, failure is the pathway that leads directly to our success. It is how you respond to failure that determines whether you benefit from it or are destroyed by it.

I had to overcome the fear of failure just like everyone else who has attempted to do great tasks. One of the most important realizations I had was that the only way to avoid failure was to do nothing. Then, of course, I would have been a complete failure! Failure is not missing the goal—failure is having no goal to miss. Failure is not losing the fight—failure is not having anything for which to fight.

Dr. Benjamin Mays, former president of Morehouse College, said, "The tragedy in life doesn't lie in not reaching your goal. The tragedy lies in having no goal to reach."[1] So if you seek to avoid failure by doing nothing, you have already failed!

So how do you make failure work for you? First, you must realize that failure simply reminds you that you are normal. Everyone we know has failed at something. Second, you realize that your failure did not kill you. The fact that you are still alive after you fail means there is something worse that could have happened to you than failure. And finally, you consider the reasons you failed and factor them into your strategy during your next attempt.

Don't give up—the last day is almost here. Keep building your plan and do not let the fear of failure stop you from going forward.

## ACTION ITEMS

1. Now is the time to retrieve the envelope you gave someone on day 1. Read the goal you wrote and reflect. Has your goal changed or stayed the same? Are you closer to achieving that goal? What are your next steps?

2. Identify a personal failure and describe what you learned from that failure.

## NOTE

1. Benjamin E. Mays, *Disturbed about Man* (Richmond, VA: John Knox, 1969), 120.

## DAY 29

# KEEP THE FAITH

*Without faith it is impossible to please God, because
anyone who comes to him must believe that he exists
and that he rewards those who earnestly seek him.*

Hebrews 11:6

One day one of my sons taught me an important lesson about faith. While I was shaving in the bathroom, my older son told me he needed money to take the train to New York and have lunch while he was there. After we negotiated the amount he needed, I agreed to fund his venture of the day.

I was sure he would come back into the bathroom to confirm our agreement. But contrary to my expectations, about twenty minutes later I received a text message informing me he was almost at the train station and he would need the money I had promised to get on the train in a few minutes. Other than wondering how my own dad would have responded had I left our house without saying good-bye, I appreciated the lesson my son had taught me about faith.

In his young mind, the commitment I had made to him required no further discussion. Without having any of the money I had agreed to provide, my son had gotten dressed, left the house, and made his way to the train station. He was so sure I would keep my word that he had proceeded with his plans as if he had already received the cash. That is what I call faith!

Faith is when you proceed with your plans without any empirical evidence that your plans are possible. Believing your plans have gained divine approval and they represent exactly what you should be doing with your life should propel you into the execution of your plans even before you have what you need to accomplish your goals.

I once spent an entire summer in church speaking about "getting to the next level." I wasn't quite sure what that meant for my own life, but I was committed to getting to the next level myself even as I served my members. Little did I know when I ventured into this uncharted territory that God would use my younger cousin to contribute to my work and take me to my next level.

My cousin had been taking courses to earn a PhD in distance learning and online education. Given the growth of our congregation and the distances people were traveling, offering Bible study and educational classes online was a next-level step for our church and my ministry. My cousin taught me how to launch my first online class and helped me manage three more online classes, which I taught at a seminary. This all happened right after I had challenged my church members to allow God to use them more than they had previously done. I was accepting my own challenge to function in a way I had never imagined.

Faith is taking action even before knowing the action will yield the desired results. Faith is setting goals even though present circumstances suggest that nothing better will ever happen. Faith is forging into the future although everything about the past argues against it.

Some people have challenged me about my faith in God. Sometimes they will say, "How do you know there is a God?" In response I say, "How do you know there is *not* a God?" Faith is choosing to believe what you believe even if it makes no sense to others.

"Faith is confidence in what we hope for and assurance about what we do not see" (Heb. 11:1). Keep the faith!

## ACTION ITEMS

1. How will you keep the faith even when circumstances make it seem as if your goals are unattainable?

2. Post this quote where you will see it frequently (on your refrigerator, the mirror in your bathroom, your computer, etc.) and use it to fuel your fire: "Faith is taking action even before knowing that the action will yield the desired results. Faith is setting goals even though present circumstances suggest that nothing better will ever happen. Faith is forging into the future although everything about the past argues against it."

## DAY 30

# PLANS ARE NOT ENOUGH

*As the body without the spirit is dead, so
faith without deeds is dead.*

James 2:26

You are now two days away from the end of your makeover month. You are two days away from blastoff. The most important lesson I have learned about planning to grow is that the very process of planning for growth *creates* growth. In the fall of 1999, Coretta Scott King, widow of Martin Luther King Jr., invited me to speak at the 2000 Martin Luther King Jr. Holiday Commemorative Celebration in Atlanta, Georgia. While conversing with her about Dr. King and his work, Mrs. King told me that her husband believed the greatest contribution made by the civil rights movement was its positive impact on the psyche of black people and all of America. That meant once a person makes up his or her mind to reject the status quo and initiates efforts toward achieving something better, that person has already grown and improved. In other words, the effort involved in creating change actually represents an internal change before the external becomes a reality. It's the renewal of our minds that ignites real transformation!

In my book *Say Yes to No Debt*, I describe debt-free living as starting when you make a commitment to debt-free living. In Romans 12 the apostle Paul said that we should "be transformed by the renewing of [our] mind" (v. 2). If you have begun to think about the future differently, then the future has already changed for you.

But planning and thinking are not enough. You must go back to the goals you have created for yourself and make sure these are actually the goals you plan to pursue. Then you should create specific steps to take in order to reach your goals. These steps become your process—and getting there does require a process.

Then you must complete your time charts to make sure every hour of the day is spent intentionally and is aligned with your goals. One of my key mottoes is this: "If you want something you have never had, you must do something you have never done." Make sure you have included in your plans doing at least one thing that is new for you. It may surprise you, but it will not take long for you to *have* something new also.

As one great philosopher once said, "Just do it!"

## ACTION ITEMS

1. Revisit and revise your goal and time charts.

2. In your plans, include at least one thing that is new for you—such as a new goal, a new strategy for achieving your goals, or a new way to find time to rest.

# DAY 31

# PRAYER CHANGES THINGS

*Pray continually.*

1 Thessalonians 5:17

Today ends the thirty-one-day journey you have ventured on to prepare for your new beginnings. Some people wait for special occasions to make new commitments. While birthdays and New Year's Day lend themselves to reflection and projection, I believe every day is a notable occasion, and therefore every day lends itself to new visions and new plans.

The most important activity to remember as you move ahead and improve your life is *prayer*. There is a spiritual aspect of life that is both unavoidable and central to who you are. Prayer enables your physical existence to actually give way to your spiritual existence so you can focus completely on the spiritual. Prayer not only summons God's assistance in your pursuit of greater things but also reminds you that you are not equipped, in your human strength, with all the resources you need to become the person you have the potential to become.

The old folks used to say, "Prayer changes things." I have learned that the first thing prayer changes is the person doing the praying.

Today, reflect on the biggest changes you have experienced since day 1. I hope you have experienced a positive shift and a complete success story.

Once you have considered your thirty-one-day journey, be prepared to start the process over! That is the strength of this workbook. You can reuse these same strategies as you continue to achieve goals or tweak existing goals based on your life circumstances. The more you practice these strategies, the better you become at turning your dreams into a reality.

I will be praying for you as you travel beyond your thirty-one-day journey. I will pray that God will bless your plans, your dreams, and your goals. And I will pray that you will remember to pray for yourself.

## ACTION ITEMS

1.  Congratulations—you did it! Reflect on this thirty-one-day makeover process. List ways in which you know you have grown over the past month.

2.  In what ways can you now say yes to life, even if it is saying no?

3.  Think about what you want to accomplish next. Describe how you will use this workbook to help you with future goal setting and achieving.

# APPENDIX

## GOAL CHART

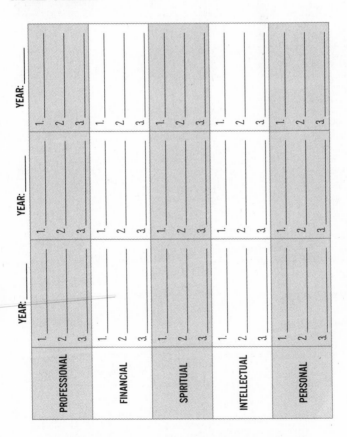

# WEEKLY ONE-HOUR TIME CHART

|         | SUN | MON | TUES | WED | THUR | FRI | SAT |
|---------|-----|-----|------|-----|------|-----|-----|
| 6 AM    |     |     |      |     |      |     |     |
| 7 AM    |     |     |      |     |      |     |     |
| 8 AM    |     |     |      |     |      |     |     |
| 9 AM    |     |     |      |     |      |     |     |
| 10 AM   |     |     |      |     |      |     |     |
| 11 AM   |     |     |      |     |      |     |     |
| 12 PM   |     |     |      |     |      |     |     |
| 1 PM    |     |     |      |     |      |     |     |
| 2 PM    |     |     |      |     |      |     |     |
| 3 PM    |     |     |      |     |      |     |     |
| 4 PM    |     |     |      |     |      |     |     |
| 5 PM    |     |     |      |     |      |     |     |
| 6 PM    |     |     |      |     |      |     |     |
| 7 PM    |     |     |      |     |      |     |     |
| PM      |     |     |      |     |      |     |     |
|         |     |     |      |     |      |     |     |
|         |     |     |      |     |      |     |     |
|         |     |     |      |     |      |     |     |

# PRIORITIES BRACKET

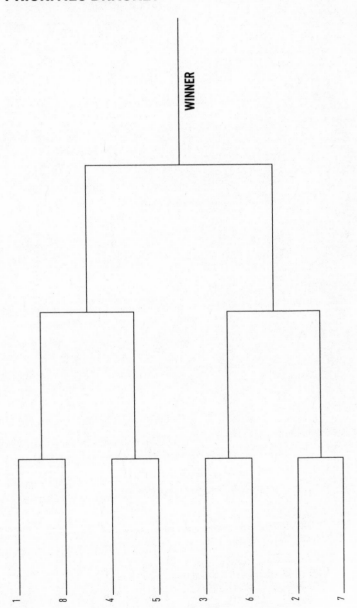